Political Humor
in America

Edited by
Stephen M. Forman

*The donkey has been a symbol of the Democratic Party since
Andrew Jackson's presidential campaign in 1828. The elephant,
symbolizing the Republican Party, was first used in 1874.*

(Courtesy of Facts Plus: An Amanack of Essential Information, *Instructional
Resources Company, Anchorage, Alaska*

Discovery Ente␣
Carlisle, Massachusetts

© Discovery Enterprises, Ltd., Carlisle, MA, 1998

ISBN 1-57960-020-4 paperback edition
Library of Congress Catalog Card Number 97-78306

10   9   8   7 6   5   4   3   2   1
Printed in the United States of America

Subject Reference Guide:

Political Humor in America
edited by Stephen M. Forman

Humor — U.S. History

Politicians — U. S. History

Photos/Illustrations:

All photos and paintings courtesy of the National Archives

Table of Contents

Introduction

by Stephen M. Forman

Political humor is like energy: once created, it cannot be destroyed, it can only change shapes. What one congressman swears is an original joke has been told countless times over the years, with different audiences, but with the same results — laughter. Take the one about the campaigning candidate who asks for another piece of chicken at a fundraiser and is told that each person is only allowed one piece. "Do you know who I am?" asks the politician. "I'm Congressman Jones." "Do you know who I am?" responds the waiter. "I'm the man in charge of the chicken." This story has been told for more than one hundred years, with slightly different twists.

This anthology has some stories and anecdotes that were meant to be funny and others that were not. Some, when they were originally told or acted out were deadly serious, but over the years we see them in a different light; taken out of their original contexts, they become funny. Examples include transcripts from *The Congressional Record* which speak for themselves. Remember, Senators and Congressmen stood on the floor of their respective Houses and uttered these words for the public record.

Beloved humorists like H. L. Mencken and Will Rogers poked fun at the political establishment through humor. Selected writings of theirs are included. As we move toward the twenty-first century new media becomes available. What was once expressed through newspaper editorials, poems, anecdotes, and oral stories now includes radio and television, comics, movies, theater productions, and, more recently, E-mail and the Internet.

But remember, there really isn't anything new under the sun. As one astute newspaper reporter said many years ago, "political jokes usually get elected."

Congress

The Congress of the United States is comprised of 535 members. Like any large group, some people are smarter than others, some are better speakers than others, and some are more humorous. Below is a sampling of their remarks and behavior covering a period of many years, following some astute comments by Will Rogers.

Will Rogers

Will Rogers, star of Broadway and the movies in the 1920s and 1930s, was also a syndicated newspaper columnist and a popular broadcaster. In his columns he told the truth in simple, often humorous ways. In the following excerpts, his grammar and style are unchanged from the orginals. His most famous quote was "I never met a man I didn't like."

Capitol Comedy Company

Source: Donald Day, editor, *The Autobiography of Will Rogers*, February 18, 1922 (Boston: Houghton Mifflin Company, 1949), pp. 77-78.

...They have what they call Congress, or the Lower House. That compares to what we call the Scenario Department. That's where somebody gets the idea of what he thinks will make a good Comedy Bill or Law, and they argue around and put it into shape.

Then it is passed along, printed, or shot, or Photographed, as we call it; then it reaches the Senate or the Cutting and Titling Department. Now in our Movie Studios we have what we call Gag Men whose sole business is to just furnish some little Gag, or Amendment as they call it, which will get a laugh or perhaps change the whole thing around.

Now the Senate has what is considered the best and highest priced Gag men that can be collected anywhere. Why, they put in so many little gags or amendments that the poor Author of the thing don't know his own story.

They consider if a man can sit there in the Studio in Washington and just put in one funny amendment in each Bill, or production, that will change it from what it originally meant, why, he is considered to have earned his pay.

Now, Folks, why patronize California-made Productions? The Capitol Comedy Co. of Washington, D.C. have never made a failure. They are every one, 100 percent funny, or 100 percent sad.

An Open Book

Source: *Ibid.*, October 21,1922, p. 86.

There's the one thing no Nation can ever accuse us of and that is Secret Diplomacy — Our Foreign dealings are an Open Book, generally a Check Book.

Party Differences

Source: *Ibid.*, October 19, 1924, p. 99.

I been trying to read the papers and see just what it is in this election that one Party wants that the other one don't. To save my soul I can't find a difference. The only thing that I can see where they differ is that the Democrats want the Republicans to get out and let them in, and the Republicans don't want to get out.

They are so hard up for an issue that Mr. Coolidge has finally just announced his policy will be Common Sense. Well, don't you know the Democrats claim that too? Do you think they will call their campaign "Darn Foolishness?" Besides, Common Sense is not an Issue in Politics, it's an affliction.

Davis announced that his Policy will be Honesty. Neither is that an issue in Politics. It's a Miracle, and can he get enough people that believe in Miracles to elect him?

The only thing I see now that the two old line Parties are divided on is "Who will have the Post offices?" No matter how many Parties you have they are all fighting for the same thing SALARY. You abolish salaries and you will abolish Politics and TAXES.

Getting New Material

Source: *Ibid.*, June 8, 1924, pp. 96-97.

I am to go into Ziegfeld's new Follies and I have no Act. So I thought I will run down to Washington and get some new material. Most people and Actors appearing on the Stage have some Writers to write their material, or they reproduce some Book or old masterpiece, but I don't do that: Congress is good enough for me.

Why should I go and pay some famous Author, or even myself to sit down all day trying to dope out something funny to say on the Stage! No Sir, I have found that there is nothing as funny as things that have happened, and that people know that have happened. So I just have them mail me everyday *The Congressional Record.* It is to me what the *Police Gazette* used to be to the fellow who was waiting for a Hair Cut, it is a life saver.

Besides, nothing is so funny as something done in seriousness. The material on which *The Congressional Record* is founded is done here every day in all seriousness. Each State elects the most serious man it has in the District, and he is impressed with the fact that he is leaving Home with the expressed idea that he is to rescue his District from Certain Destruction, and to see that it receives its just amount of Rivers and Harbors, Post Offices, and Pumpkin Seeds. Naturally you have put a pretty big load on that Man. I realize that it is no joking matter to be grabbed up bodily from the Leading Lawyer's Office of Main Street and have the entire Populace tell you what is depending on you when you get to Washington. The Fellow may be all right personally and a good fellow, but that Big League Idea of Politics just kinder scares him.

Now, they wouldn't be so serious and particular if they only had to vote on what they thought was good for the Majority of the people of the U.S. That would be a Cinch. But what makes it hard for them is that every time a Bill comes up they have a million things to decide that have nothing to do with the merit of the Bill. They first must consider is, or was, it introduced by a member of the opposite Political Party. If it is, why then something is wrong with it from the start, for everything the opposite does has a catch in it. Then the principal thing is of course, "what will this do for me personally back home?" If it is something that he thinks the folks back home may never read, or hear of, why then he can vote any way he wants to, but Politics and Self-Preservation must come first, never mind, the majority of the people of the U.S. If Lawmakers were elected for Life, I believe they would do better. A man's thoughts are naturally on his next term, more than on his Country.

Outside the Congress Hall, they are as fine a bunch of men as any one ever met in his life. They are full of Humor and regular fellows. That is, as I say, when you catch them when they haven't got Politics on their Minds. But the minute they get in that immense Hall they begin to get Serious, and it's then that they do such Amusing Things. If we could just send the same bunch of men to Washington for the Good of the Nation, and not for Political Reasons, we could have the most perfect Government in the world.

Professional Joke Makers

It may interest you to know that five of Will Rogers' articles have been read on the floor of Congress and printed in The Congressional Record *as representing a typical American view of important public subjects.*

Source: *Ibid.*, pp. 111-112.

When a Gentleman quoted me on the floor of Congress the other day, another member took exception and said he objected to the remarks of a Professional Joke Maker going into *The Congressional Record.*

Now can you beat that for jealousy among people in the same line? Call me a Professional Joke Maker! He is right about everything but the Professional. THEY are the Professional Joke Makers. Read some of the Bills that they have passed, if you think they ain't Joke makers. I could study all my life and not think up half the amount of funny things they can think of in one Session of Congress. Besides my jokes don't do anybody any harm. You don't have to pay any attention to them. But everyone of the jokes those Birds make is a LAW and hurts somebody (generally everybody).

"Joke Maker!" He couldn't have coined a better term for Congress if he had been inspired. But I object to being called a Professional. I am an Amateur beside them. If I had that Guy's unconscious Humor, Ziegfield couldn't afford to pay me I would be so funny.

Of course I can understand what he was objecting to was any common Sense creeping into *The Record.* It was such a Novelty, I guess it did sound funny.

And, by the way, I have engaged counsel and if they ever put any more of my material in that "Record of Inefficiency" I will start suit for deformation [sic] of Character. I don't want my stuff buried away where Nobody ever reads it. I am not going to lower myself enough to associate with them in a Literary way.

The Congressional Record

The Congressional Record *is a verbatim transcript of what happens each day on the floors of the Senate and House of Representatives. At times it is tedious reading, but at other times the exchanges between members is very interesting and very funny. The following excerpts are taken directly from* The Congressional Record.

The Congressman's Pay

Source: *The Congressional Record*, Senator Quenrin Burdick (D-N.D.), January 29, 1987.

Mr. BURDICK. I would like to Conclude with the thoughts of one of my constituents, Mr. Bill Snyder, of Fargo, ND. Mr. Snyder dared me to include his poem in *THE CONGRESSIONAL RECORD*. Well, here it goes, Mr.Snyder.

> Chop the old folks,
> Cut the young,
> Slice the budget,
> Rung by rung.
> But never, never,
> Vote away,
> Any boost
> in Congressman's pay!

An Amendment to an Amendment to the Original Amendment?

Sometimes, the language becomes as confusing as the Abbott and Costello "bit" known commonly as "Who's on first?"

Source: *Ibid.*, Representatives Don Fuqua (D-Fla) and Gerry E. Studds (D-Mass) (Presiding Officer), October 18, 1979.

Mr. FUQUA. Mr. Chairman, I have a parliamentary inquiry.

The Chairman pro tempore [temporary chairman]. The Chair will advise Members that there is a reasonably complex situation before the Committee. To attempt to elucidate it, we must have order. The Chair will advise the gentleman from Florida the order in which the questions will be put. The gentleman from Florida [Mr. FUQUA] will state his parliamentary inquiry.

Mr. FUQUA. Mr. Chairman, prior to the recent vote there was an amendment offered by the gentleman from Pennsylvania [Mr. KOSTMAYER] to the amendment offered by the gentleman from Washington [Mr. McCORMACK] as a substitute for the amendment offered by the gentleman from Pennysylvania [Mr. KOSTMAYER] as modified. Somewhere along the line I had an amendment to the Kostmayer amendment. Could the Chair state the parliamentary situation and the sequence in which the votes will occur?

The CHAIRMAN pro tempore. The Chair will attempt to do so. The Chair will inform the Committee that all time has expired. The order in which the votes will be put is as follows: The first vote will occur on the amendment offered by the gentleman from Florida [Mr. FUQUA] to the amendment offered by the gentleman from Pennsylvania [Mr. KOSTMAYER] as modified. The second vote will occur on the amendment offered by the gentleman from Pennsylvania [Mr. KOSTMAYER] to the amendment offered by the gentleman from Washington [Mr. McCORMACK] as a substitute for the amendment offered by the gentleman from Pennsylvania [Mr. KOSTMAYER] as modified. The third vote will occur on the amendment offered by the gentleman from Washington [Mr. McCORMACK] as a substitute for the amendment offered by the gentleman from Pennsylvania [Mr. KOSTMAYER] as modified and the final vote will be the original Kostmayer amendment as amended. The Chair will now put the question....

A Bicentennial Fruit Salad

Although serious business is often conducted, sometimes things get out-of-hand on the floor of the House.

Source: *Ibid.*, Representative Richard Kelly (R-Fla), February 17, 1976.

Mr. KELLY. Mr. Speaker, it is with reluctance I oppose and expose a plot among four very respected members of this House — Mr. ROBINSON of Virginia, Mr. McCORMACK of Washington, Mr. GOODLING of Pennsylvania, and Mr. SYMMS of Idaho. Apples are grown in their states.

And these men are out to upset our apple carts. Their recent actions show they want the whole bite of the apple for their constituents. They are part of the Big Apple cartel.

They have introduced a resolution naming the apple The Official Bicentennial Fruit and will ask this House to approve it. Their motives are exclusionary and certainly contrary to the spirit of the Revolution.

They trample on the customs of this venerable House, Mr. Speaker. They count apples and forget to tell us apples cannot be compared to oranges. I am here to say very little can compare with oranges.

To officially make the munching of an apple an act of patriotism is serious business. It will change our American way of life, Mr. Speaker. They are meddling. They could have all Hawaii's pineapple growers on the dole. Things would no longer be peaches and cream in Georgia. They might even try to declare life is nothing but a bowl of apples. These comments are not sour grapes, my fellow Members of California and New York, but recognition of a clear and present danger. Their plotting is going to get us into a jam, a pickle.

These men imply apples were the first fruit brought to these shores. They claim America and apples are synonymous and that apples are the most popular and widey grown fruit in the United States.

All of that is so much applesauce.

I tell you, this power play by the Big Apple interests is rotten to the core.

Who, among the great orators in this House, ever speaks in apple-shaped tones? Who would feel comfortable with apples jubilee? Could anyone be so unaware of our heritage as to ask Billy Boy if she can bake an apple pie? Would many be so untraditional as to set a Thanksgiving table without cranberry sauce?

A popular variety of orange is the Parson Brown, Mr. Speaker. It is sweet to the palate and refreshing to the soul. Now, I ask you, what is more American than the name Parson Brown? Or just roll the word Valencia off your tongue. It makes you feel majestic to say it. It is an orange. Winesap is harsh to the ear. It is an apple.

Our orange blossom is the symbol of newlywed bliss. All the Big Apples have to offer is a song, "Don't Sit Under the Apple Tree With Anyone Else But Me," which is a wartime plea for fidelity. Are they trying to lead this Nation further down the road of permissiveness? Surely all of us recall what Eve started with the apple.

True, the apple has wormed its way into our folklore — things tend to be in apple pie order and as American as apple pie. But the apple has had good public relations since the days of Johnny Appleseed. They want you to forget one rotten apple spoils the barrel. And it may be true an apple a day keeps the doctor away. But have you ever heard of anyone suffering the green apricot trots? Only apples can do that for you.

They keep quiet what Herman Melville said in his masterwork, *Moby Dick*: "Hell is an idea first born on an undigested apple dumpling."

Rather than give us full disclosure, they lull us with endearments: "apple of my eye" and "sweeter than apple cider."

I sincerely hope my well-intended remarks do not earn me the reputation of being antiapple. I extend the olive branch. The apple is a noble fruit. I like it. I have them in my home. They are among the good things in life. They were of great importance in the settlement of this country. But just as this Nation had many founding fathers, it had many founding fruits.

But these men have shown they don't care a fig for the rest of us. As sure as God made little green apples, the sponsors of this resolution are about to offend the spirit that made America what it is today.

More fitting, Mr. Speaker, would be a resolution declaring the fruit salad our Bicentennal Appetizer. It would encourage dietary patriotism, in the interest of national unity, while avoiding potential widespread agricultural unemployment.

I believe this discourse has gone to the meat of the coconut. Let us not buy a lemon. Let us preserve ourselves. Let us remember how our gardens grow.

Prime Farmland

Source: *Ibid.*, Senators Charles Percy (R-Ill) and Clifford Hansen (R-Wyo), May 20, 1977.

Mr. PERCY. Mr. President, will the Senator yield an appropriate point for a question?

Mr. HANSEN. I am happy to yield.

Mr. PERCY. Senator CULVER began his colloquy on the question of whether or not we can define what prime farmland is. I just wonder whether the Senator from Wyoming can now go back to his constituents and feel properly equipped to define and explain what primary farmland is.

16

Mr. HANSEN. The Senator uses the word "primary" as I understood him. He means "prime" does he not?

Mr. PERCY. This is correct, prime farmland.

Mr. HANSEN. A very simple answer to the Senator's question is, no, I could not.

Mr. PERCY. May this Senator put it in very simple terms, then, so my distinguished colleague could go back to his State and explain it? It is soils having aquic or udic moisture regimes; or soils having xeric or ustic moisture regimes.

If the farmer does not understand that, we could say soils having aridic or torric moisture regimes. If we want to be more specific, we could say soils have a soil temperature regime that is frigid, mesic, thermic, or hyperthermic — that is, pergelic or cryic regimes are excluded; or, soils with zero horizon which is higher than 47 degrees Fahrenheit or 8 degrees Centigrade.

If the farmer wants to have further explanation, I would go on to tell him then, as an expert in the field, that soils having a pH between 4.5 and 8.4 in all horizons within a depth of 40 inches would qualify, or that the conductivity of saturation extract that is less than 4 mmhos/cm and the exchangeable sodium percentage — that is, ESP — is less than 15....

Mr. HANSEN. Mr. President, I appreciate the always generous impulses of my good friend from Illinois....

I have to say that I do not propose to go out to Wyoming and respond to a question of what is prime farmland using some of this language. I am afraid I might get socked in the nose. They might misunderstand what I am trying to say when I use the words the Senator pronounces so easily and which I am afraid I would stumble over. They might even think I am calling them a bad name.

Radios

Source: *Ibid.*, Senator Cole L. Blease (D-S.C.), March 1, 1929.

Mr. BLEASE. Now they want to put a radio back here right behind me so as to broadcast what is going on in the Senate. I do not know anything about radios; I never listened to one of them in my life. I do not know what they might do, and that is what I want to ask the Senators. What danger might lurk in such an instrument, for instance, at the time of the inauguration, now only three days distant? They might fill that thing up with gas, some deadly gas, and just about the time the crowd assembled in this chamber, everybody in control of the government of the United States, some fellow might turn on a machine down here and just gas out the whole business.

I do not care very much about the radio bill. I will be honest about it. I am opposed to it. I was the only man who voted against it when it came up. I have rather peculiar ideas, I guess, and perhaps a lot of people think they are fool ideas. I suppose some would put a "d" in front of that word to better express the kind of ideas they think I have. But to save my life I can not see what right we have to control the air that God Almighty gave the people.

Santa Claus

Source: *Ibid.*, Representative Steven D. Symms (R-Idaho), December 20, 1974.

Mr. SYMMS. Mr. Speaker, rumors are flying around Washington to the effect that this may have been Santa Claus' last year of operation. Sources within the federal bureaucracy are privately indicating that the jolly old man is in big, big trouble.

Apparently, from the Federal Government's point of view, Santa has been "getting away with murder" for years now, "breaking every law in the book," as they put it. And indeed, the time has come to crack down on this unconscionable situation.

Here is the inside scoop on Santa's long list of infractions:

First. Operating a flying sleigh in absence of certification by the Civil Aeronautics Board, a clear violation of the Civil Aeronautics Act of 1938.

Second. Unlawfully competing with the U.S. Postal Service on air mail deliveries.

Third. Violating Environmental Protection Agency's requirements for emissions control devices on his reindeer.

Fourth. Breaking the Sherman Antitrust Act by mintaining a strict monopoly in his profession.

Fifth. Violating the Fair Labor Standards Act by failing to pay his elves the minimum wage on proper overtime benefits.

Sixth. Engaging in unfair promotional advertising, designed to prey on the defenseless minds of children, a violation of Trade Commission regulations.

Seventh. Failing to secure an Interstate Commerce Commission permit and an assignment of certified routes by the Interstate Commerce Commission.

Eighth. Violating numerous Occupational Safety and Health Administration — OSHA — regulations by operating an "unsafe workplace."

Ninth. Passing out candy canes and goodies not approved by the Food and Drug Administration.

Tenth. Ignoring the edicts of the Equal Employment Opportunity Commission and the Civil Rights Act of 1964 by failing to institute a quota system in his workshop based on race, religion, sex, and size — too many elves.

Eleventh. Making toys which were not approved by the Consumer Product Safety Commission.

Twelfth. Failing to declare the cookies and milk which are out for him as taxable income with the Internal Revenue Service.

Thirteenth. Transporting firearms across State lines as Christmas presents.

Fourteenth. Avoiding State and Federal taxes on his sleigh, not to mention licensing, registration, and having an operator's permit.

Fifteenth. Making various infractions of National Labor Relations Board regulations, including the maintenance of a nonunion shop and unfairly competing with the chimney sweeps' union.

Mr. Speaker, it is said that these are but a sampling of Santa's more serious Federal offenses, which taken in total, will almost certainly put the man out of business for good.

What The Heck

Source: *Ibid.*, Representatives Bob Eckhardt (D-Texas) and Andrew Jacobs, Jr. (D-Ind), June 12, 1975.

Mr. ECKHARDT. Mr. Chairman, as I understand what the gentleman is doing, the amendment is saying that 4 years after any particular mileage standard required for an entire fleet of cars, then there may not be any car distributed which exceeds that figure to which the limitation was placed 4 years earlier on the entire fleet, and if it is attempted to sell a car which does not meet that standard, the company may be enjoined from selling it?

Mr. JACOBS. By action of the Justice Department; the gentleman is right.

Mr. ECKHARDT. And in addition to that, this only applies to passenger vehicles; is that correct?

Mr. JACOBS. Well, I do not know just what that means — but yes, what the heck.

New Mexico

Source: *Ibid.*, Senators Pete V. Domenici (R-N. Mex), Warren Rudman (R-N.H.), Rudy Boschwitz (R-Minn), Russell B. Long (D-La), and Alan K. Simpson (R-Wyo), June 13, 1986.

Mr. DOMENICI. Mr. President, I shortly shall send to the desk for its immediate consideration, and I ask unanimous consent that it be in order to do so, a resolution that will recognize today, June 13, 1986 as "New Mexico is a State Day." This resolution is necessary to draw attention to a reality that is frequently overlooked, either through ignorance or hearing impairment.

I ask my colleagues in the Senate to recognize that New Mexico is a state.

I ask that my colleagues recognize that I was not sent to Washington, along with my distinguished junior Senator, Senator Jeff Bingaman, from a foreign country but from a State of the Union. We were both elected by U.S. citizens who reside in the sovereign State of New Mexico. For those who are not familiar with the geographic location of my State, the Land of Enchantment, it is directly south of Colorado, east of Arizona, west of Texas, and north of the Mexican border. I repeat, north of the Mexican border. I repeat, north of the Mexican border. It was established as the 47th State in the Union in 1912.

Recently, a congressional candidate, David Cargo, a former Governor of my State, was informed by the Treasury Department that 30 percent of his Treasury Bills would be withheld because he lived in a foreign country....

Mr. President, this is not the first time that New Mexico has suffered an identity crisis at the hands of the Federal Government. The State Department has been known to refer my staff to its foreign affairs desk. Grocery and drug stores in Washington have refused to honor New Mexico drivers' licenses, stating that it is their store's policy to take checks only from American citizens. When individuals are planning vacations in my beautiful State, there are frequent inquiries concerning visas, immunization, and the relative drinkability of our water. There are 1.3 million people who reside in the beautiful and sovereign State of New Mexico, fifth largest State of the Union, by area. There are no horses that are tied to hitching posts on Main Street. In fact, we have removed most of the hitching posts from most of our cities. We use U.S. currency, not pesos.

In this resolution, which I am joined by my good friend,

Senator BINGAMAN, who is also from New Mexico, elected by American citizens, we have summarized all the things we are, all the things our State stands for, and some of the things we have contributed to our national well-being. We now send this resolution to the desk and ask for its immediate consideration.....

Mr. RUDMAN addressed the chair.

The PRESIDING OFFICER. The Senator from New Mexico.

Mr. RUDMAN. I wonder if my friend from New Mexico would yield for a question.

Mr. DOMENICI. I would be pleased to yield to my good friend.

Mr. RUDMAN. I find it very hard to believe that the Department of the Treasury would have made such a grievous error, and I wonder whether or not, the Senator from New Mexico might not be missing something.

As the chairman of the Budget Committee, is it possible that because of Graham-Rudman [an Act that led to Federal deficit reductions and the requirement of a balanced budget by 1991 — editor] we have eliminated New Mexico?

Mr. DOMENICI. Well, I plan to leave here in about 45 minutes to go up to the Senator's State. I thought I was going up there to pay him honor and homage. I guarantee I would not be going up there if Graham-Rudman eliminated us as a State of the United States.

Mr. RUDMAN. Will my friend yield for just one last question? I wonder if my friends from New Mexico might have considered that there might be some advantages to allowing this situation to ripen. After all, if you were expelled from the Union, I expect the Senator from New Mexico would immediately ask for a large block of foreign aid money.

Mr. DOMENICI. Let me say to my good friend, the fate of foreign aid in the national budget is not better than any of the other expenditures. I do not think we would be any better off. But perhaps we will ask New Mexicans if they want to consider that alternative.

Mr. RUDMAN. There is always the other alternative of a foreign military sales agreement with this administration. I expect that the people of New Mexico might like Stinger missiles, Sidewinder missles, and even Harpoon missiles to defend the vast ocean spaces of the State of New Mexico....

The Differences between Republicans and Democrats

Source: *Ibid.*, Representative Andrew Jacobs, Jr. (D-Ind), July 19, 1983.

Mr. JACOBS. Mr. Speaker, the following is circa early 1960s, but it probably remains about right.

Although to the casual glance Republicans and Democrats may appear to be almost indistinguishable, here are some hints which should result in positive identification.

Democrats seldom make good polo players. They would rather listen to Bela Bartok.

The people you see coming out of white wooden churches are Republicans.

Democrats buy most of the books that have been banned somewhere. Republicans form censorship committees and read them as a group.

Republicans are likely to have fewer but larger debts that cause them no concern.

Democrats owe a lot of small bills. They don't worry either.

24

Republicans consume three-fourths of all the rutabaga produced in this country. The remainder is thrown out.

Republicans usually wear hats and almost always clean their paintbrushes.

Democrats give their worn-out clothes to those less fortunate. Republicans wear theirs.

Republicans post all the signs saying No Trespassing and These Deer are Private Property and so on. Democrats bring picnic baskets and start their bonfires with signs.

Republicans employ exterminators. Democrats step on the bugs.

Republicans have governesses for their children. Democrats have grandmothers.

Democrats name their children after currently popular sports figures, politicians, and entertainers. Republican children are named after their parents or grandparents, according to where the most money is.

Large cities such as New York are filled with Republicans — up until 5 p.m. At this point there is a phenomenon much like an automatic washer starting the spin cycle. People begin pouring out of every exit of the city. These are Republicans going home.

Democrats keep trying to cut down on smoking, but are not successful. Neither are Republicans.

Republicans tend to keep their shades drawn, although there is seldom any reason why they should. Democrats ought to, but don't.

Republicans fish from the stern of a chartered boat. Democrats sit on the dock and let the fish come to them.

Republicans study the financial pages of the newspaper. Democrats put them in the bottom of the bird cage.

Most of the stuff you see alongside the road has been thrown out of car windows by Democrats.

On Saturday, Republicans head for the hunting lodge or the yacht club. Democrats wash the car and get a haircut.

Republicans raise dahlias, Dalmatians, and eyebrows. Democrats raise Airedales, kids, and taxes.

Democrats eat the fish they catch. Republicans hang them on the wall.

Democrats watch TV crime and Western shows that make them clench their fists and become red in the face. Republicans get the same effect from the Presidential press conferences.

Christmas cards that Democrats send are filled with reindeer and chimneys and long messages. Republicans select cards containing a spray of holly, or a single candle.

Democrats are continually saying, "This Christmas we're going to be sensible." Republicans consider this highly unlikely.

Republicans smoke cigars on weekdays.

Republicans have guest rooms. Democrats have spare rooms filled with old baby furniture.

Republican boys date Democratic girls. They plan to marry Republican girls, but feel they're entitled to a little fun first.

Democrats make up plans and then do something else. Republicans follow the plans their grandfathers made.

Democrats purchase all the tools — the power saws and mowers. A Republican probably wouldn't know how to use a screwdriver.

Democrats suffer from chapped hands and headaches. Republicans have tennis elbow and gout.

Republicans sleep in twin beds — some even in separate rooms. That is why there are more Democrats.

Chili

Source: *Ibid.*, Senators John Tower (R-Tex), Barry Goldwater (R-Ariz), and Robert C. Byrd (D-W Va), February 5, 1974.

Mr. TOWER obtained the floor.

Mr. GOLDWATER. Mr. President, a parliamentary inquiry, Will the Senator from Texas use his microphone? If he is going to insult me, I want to hear it.

Mr. TOWER. Mr. President. I note from an article in the Houston *Chronicle* of this past weekend that the junior Senator from Arizona, the honorable BARRY GOLDWATER, apparently made some comment on Texas Chili at a function this past weekend at the National Press Club.

The *Chronicle* quoted the Arizona Senator as saying: "I have heard that the club serves only Texas chili. Tell me this is not true. A Texan does not know chili from leavings in a corral."

Now, Mr. President, if this is an accurate quote of the distinguished junior Senator from Arizona, I submit that this raises very grave questions about that Senator's taste.

The whole world knows, Mr. President that the best chili anywhere is brewed in Texas. Ask any Texan over the age of 3 months if there are any doubts lingering in the mind of anyone. Is not Texas the site for the annual world's champion chili cookoff at Terlingua? Is Texas not the home of the late chili king, Wick Fowler, whose family still packages the world-famous Two Alarm Chili at Austin? Is the Chili Appreciation Society International not headquartered at Dallas, where some of the world's foremost chili experts reside?

Comparing Arizona chili to Texas chili is like comparing Phyllis Diller to Sophia Loren....

Who Am I?

Source: *Ibid.*, Senator Howard Baker, Jr. (R-Tenn), June 23, 1983.

Mr. BAKER. Mr. President, this is the first week of summer. I do not clearly recall if we had any spring. In any event, it is nice to know that summer has arrived and with it, inevitably, the realization that we go downhill from here, as the days grow shorter from this day forward until mid-December.

Mr. President, it also means that the Capitol Building, to say nothing of the city as a whole, will look forward to the visitation of countless millions of visitors.

I always count it a great tribute to the solidarity and future of American democracy that so many Americans want to come to this city and see the monumental structures, the Capitol, the White House, the Mall, and to travel through those spaces, including the corridors of the Capitol itself.

Sometimes the throng of tourists through the Capitol corridors can become an impediment to progress. Sometimes, even, it can be an assault on one's ego.

The other day, I was walking from this Chamber back to my office, and an excited group stopped me and someone said, "Say, I know who you are. Don't tell me. Let me guess. Let me remember. I'll get it in a minute."

I waited for several seconds, and finally said, "Howard Baker." He said, "no that's not it." (laughter)

Order in the House

Source: *Ibid.*, Representative James A. Gallivan (D-Mass), February 16, 1927.

Mr. GALLIVAN submitted the following resolution; which was referred to the Committee on Rules and ordered to be printed.

H RES. 429
IN THE HOUSE OF REPRESENTATIVES
February 16, 1927

RESOLUTION

Whereas the physical exercise of hostile encounter by means of human fists is becoming of daily occurence in the House of Representatives; and,

Whereas such encounters are being conducted in an irregular manner, with small regard to race, weight, reach, height, or classification of Members to insure fair fighting; and

Whereas most of the principal communities of the United States have boxing boards or commissions, whose duty it is to regulate the sport and insure fair play; Therefore be it

Resolved, That a committee be appointed by the Speaker of the House, who shall be chairman ex officio, to be known as the Boxing Board of the House of Representatives, to have full authority in the arranging of bouts between Members according to weight, corporeal and mental age, and experience; and be it further

Resolved, That said board shall arrange to hold the bouts in Statuary Hall, under the paternal eyes of the fathers of the Republic, and under no circumstances shall said board authorize bouts either in the House of Representatives or before committees of the House unless contestants sign written agreements, approved by the chairman, to abstain from hair pulling, profanity, and tobacco chewing, and the use of wrist watches or flasks; and be it further

Resolved, That the Honorable William D. Upshaw, of Georgia, is appointed permanent referee of all bouts held under the jurisdiction of said board, his salary and expenses to be paid out of the contingent fund of the House.

The Presidency

The forty-one men who served as President of the United States came from varied backgrounds. Their occupations include lawyer, educator, farmer, soldier, businessman, entertainer, and newspaper reporter. Some were rich, some were poor; some intellectuals, some poorly educated. Some were outgoing, and some were reserved. All in all, they had diverse talents, backgrounds, strengths, and limitations. The selected collection of anecdotes and humor represents the personality of several of those Presidents, following a few words on the office from H. L. Mencken.

H. L. Mencken

Henry Louis Mencken was a newspaper reporter at the beginning of the twentieth centuy. He worked for the Baltimore Sun *for his entire professional life. As a commentator on American life, what he saw usually displeased him. He believed that the American citizen was of such a low level of intelligence that he deserved what he got. Because his writing was in comic style, he had a large following.*

Imperial Purple

Source: H. L. Mencken, *The American Scene,* Huntington Cairns (New York: Alfred A. Knopf, 1965), pp. 223-226.

1931

Most of the rewards of the Presidency, in these degenerate days, have come to be very trashy. The President continues, of course, to be an eminent man. He sees little of the really intelligent and amusing people of the country: most of them, in fact, make it sort of a point of honor to scorn him and avoid him. His time is put in mainly with shabby politicians and other such designing fellows — in brief, with rogues and ignoramuses. When he takes a little holiday his customary companions are vermin that no fastidious man would consort with — dry Senators with panting thirsts, the proprietors of bad newspapers in worse towns, grafters preying on the suffering farmers, power and movie magnates....They must be dreadful company.

The honors that are heaped upon a President in this one hundred and fifty-sixth year of the Republic are seldom of a kind to impress and content a civilized man. People send him turkeys, opossums, pieces of wood from the Constitution, goldfish, carved peach-kernels, models of the State capitols of Wyoming and Arkansas, and pressed flowers from the Holy Land....Once a year some hunter in Montana or Idaho sends him 20 pounds of bearsteak, usually collect. It arrives in a high state, and has to be fed to the White House dog. He receives 20 to 30 chain-prayer letters every day, and fair copies of 40 or 50 sets of verse. Colored clergymen send him illustrated Bibles, madstones, and boxes of lucky powders, usually accompanied by applications for appointment as collectors of customs at New Orleans, or Register of the Treasury.

...The health of the President is watched very carefully, not only by the Vice-President, but also by medical men detailed for the purpose by the Army or Navy. These medical men have high-sounding titles, and perform the duties of their office in full uniform, with swords on one side and stethoscopes on the other. The diet of their imperial patient is rigidly scrutinized. ...Every morning they look at his tongue, take his pulse and temperature, determine his blood pressure, and examine his eyegrounds and his knee-jerks. The instant he shows the slightest sign of being upset they clap him into bed, post

31

Marines to guard him, put him on a regimen fit for a Trappist, and issue bulletins to the newspapers.

...The President has less privacy than any other American. Thousands of persons have the right of access to him, beginning with the British Ambassador and running down to the secretary of the Republican county committee of Ziebach county, South Dakota. Among them are the 96 members of the United States Senate, pehaps the windiest and most tedious group of men in Christendom....Many of these gentlemen drop in, not because they have anything to say, but simply to prove to their employers or customers that they can do it.

...All day long the right honorable lord of us all sits listening solemnly to quacks who pretend to know what the farmers are thinking about in Nebraska and South Carolina, how the Swedes of Minnesota are taking the German moratorium, and how much it would cost in actual votes to let fall a word for beer and light wines. A secretary rushes in with the news that some eminent movie actor or football coach has died, and the President must seize a pen and write a telegram of condolence to the widow.

...There comes a day of public ceremonial, and a chance to make a speech. Alas, it must be made at the annual banquet of some organization that is discovered, at the last minute, to be made up mainly of gentlemen under indictment, or at the tomb of some statesman who escaped impeachment by a hair. A million voters with IQ's below 60 have their ears glued to the radio: it takes four days' hard work to concoct a speech with a sensible word in it. Next day a dam must be opened somewhere. Four dry Senators get drunk and make a painful scene. The Presidential automobile runs over a dog. It rains.

The life seems dull and unpleasant. A bootlegger has a better time, in jail or out. Yet it must have its charms, for no man who has experienced it is ever unwilling to endure it again. On the contrary, all ex-Presidents try their level best to get back, even at the expense of their dignity, their sense of humor, and their immortal souls....

Calvin Coolidge

Source: *The Fun and Laughter of Politics*, compiled by Senator John F. Parker (New York: Doubleday and Co. Inc., 1978), pp. 220-221.

Calvin Coolidge, our thirtieth President said very little, but often his words were extremely humorous in a down-home sort of way. He had no desire to be funny — it just so happened that many things he said came out that way.

Noted as a man who knew what both sides of a dollar bill looked like, Coolidge left the White House one day for a needed rest and checked into a swank hotel. When he got the bill, he was shocked. Having left a two-dollar room at the Adams House in Boston, when he was governor of Massachusetts, Coolidge could not understand the twelve-dollar rate at the Washington hotel. Fuming, he paid the bill. He then noted that he needed some stamps to send off a few letters.

"How many two-cent stamps do you want?" the clerk asked.

"Depends," replied Coolidge suspiciously. "How much are you asking for them?"

A lady reporter was interviewing President Coolidge. "What is your hobby?" she asked. "Holding office," was Cal's quick reply.

When someone asked the President how many people worked at the White House, he responded: "About half of them."

John Tyler

Source: *Ibid.*, p. 224.

When President Harrison died, Vice-President Tyler succeeded him in the White House. The new President's first act was to commission his coachman to purchase a carriage. In a few days the coachman returned and reported that he had searched Washington and found a very handsome carriage for sale, but it had been used a few times.

"That will never do," said Tyler. "It would not be proper for the President of the United States to drive around in a second-hand carriage."

"And sure," responded the old coachman, "but what are you, sir, but a second-hand President?"

Herbert Hoover

Source: *Ibid.*, pp. 226-227.

After leaving the White House, former President Hoover checked in to a Canadian resort for a needed rest. When he placed his name on the hotel register, the clerk looked at it and seemed impressed.

"Are you any relation to G-man J. Edgar Hoover?" he asked. "No," said Herbert Hoover. The clerk sized up the distinguished guest and came on again: "I suppose you're part of the Hoover family that manufactures vacuum cleaners?" Again Hoover said: "No."

"Oh well," said the hotel clerk, "that's all right. But we do get a kick out of entertaining relatives of real celebrities."

Zachary Taylor

Source: *Ibid.*, pp. 227-228.

After the Mexican War and the annexation of Texas, Southern California, New Mexico, and Arizona, President Zachary Taylor commissioned General William T. Sherman, then a captain, to look over the new possessions and see what they were worth, for they had never been surveyed.

Captain Sherman was gone for two years and during that time he penetrated every corner of the new territory. When he returned to Washington he called on the President.

"Well, Sherman," said President Taylor, "what do you think of our new possessions? Will they pay for the blood and treasure spent in the war?"

"Do you want my honest opinion?" replied Sherman.

"Yes tell us privately just what you think."

"Well, Mr. President," said Sherman "it cost us one hundred million dollars and ten thousand men to carry on the war with Mexico. "I know," said President Taylor, "but we got Arizona, New Mexico, Southern California, Texas and...."

"Oh, sure we did," interrupted Sherman, "but I've been out there and looked them over — all that country — and between me and you, I feel that we'll have to go to war again. Yes, we've got to have another war."

"For what?" asked the puzzled Taylor.

"Why to make the Mexicans take the place back again."

Lyndon Johnson

Source: *Ibid.*, p. 255.

President Johnson had a chauffeur who had served him during Johnson's days as Senate Majority Leader. When Johnson became Kennedy's Vice-President, the chauffeur had been transferred to Johnson's limousine. One day Johnson noticed that the chauffeur was becoming very grumpy. "This was strange, for my chauffeur was ordinarily a very cheerful fellow," said Johnson. "I asked him what his trouble was, and this is the way he put it." "Well, I don't mean to be personal or anything like that, but my wife thinks I ought to get a job driving somebody important."

John F. Kennedy

Source: *Ibid.*, p. 273.

President Kennedy was always being kidded about his father's money and was even accused of using his wealth to buy votes. At a dinner in Washington, the witty Kennedy confronted the accusation by saying: "I have received the following telegram from my generous father — 'Dear Jack, Don't buy a single vote more than is necessary. I'll be darned if I'm going to pay for a landslide.' "

William Taft

Source: *Ibid.*, pp. 232-233.

President Taft was a huge man, and when he walked the floors literally bent under his weight. He was the subject of many humorous stories, not the least of which was one about his visit to the home of an old friend. It was a small house and not well built. As Taft walked about, it seemed the house shook in every rafter. When Taft went to sleep that night, the bed gave way, dumping the President on the floor. His friend hurried to the door. "What's the matter, Bill?" he cried anxiously. "Oh, I'm all right, I guess," Taft good-naturedly called out to his friend, "but say, Joe, if you don't find me here in the morning, look in the cellar."

President Taft told the story about a train trip he took through the Midwest in the days when trains seldom stopped at the smaller towns. Taft had made plans to stop at a little place in Kansas to visit some friends. He was informed that the train never made special stops "except for large parties."

"Oh a large party is getting off at that station," Taft told the railroad conductor. When the conductor asked the name of the party, Taft jovially said: "It's me."

Dwight Eisenhower

Source: *Ibid.*, p. 242.

President Eisenhower was a man who had faced countless dangers over a lifetime of military service. However, when called upon to address groups of women, he became extremely nervous. To an aide he once whispered: "I'd rather face a cannon than these women."

In any event, one day he was called upon to address an organization of women meeting in Washington for a three-day convention. The President gave them the full treatment: military training, missiles, comparative strength of America versus that of her enemies, weapons, the nation's firepower, etc. In fact, it was one of his best speeches to a women's group. When he had finished he asked: "And now, are there any questions?"

A neat little lady in a green dress arose and asked: "Will you tell us why your wife Mamie always wears bangs?"

Franklin D. Roosevelt

Source: *Ibid.*, p. 243.

On one of President Franklin Roosevelt's campaign tours, he invited the mayor of a small city to ride in the open car with him. They were late for a scheduled meeting, and Roosevelt ordered the driver to speed up. As the car whirled through the center of town, the people on the sidewalks were but a blur. Finally, the mayor said: "Mr. President, do you think you should be riding so fast?" Roosevelt laughed and said: "Oh, it's all right, they know who I am."

"That may be so," responded the mayor, "but do you mind slowing up a bit so they can see who's with you?"

Thomas Jefferson

Source: Henry S. Randall, *The Life of Thomas Jefferson*, 3 volumes (New York: Derby and Jackson, 1858, Volume I), pp. 178-179.

In February 1770, when Jefferson and his mother were visiting a neighbor, one of their slaves rushed up in great excitement to report that their house at Shadwell had caught fire and that everything in it had been destroyed. "But were none of my books saved?" cried Jefferson in great distress. "No master," said the man; then he added with a smile, "But we saved the fiddle."

Source: Sarah N. Randolph, *The Domestic Life of Thomas Jefferson* (New York: Harper and Brothers, 1871), p. 49.

When Congress was discussing independence, according to a story Jefferson told a friend in his old age, meetings were held near a livery-stable, and the meeting hall was beseiged by flies. The delegates wore short breeches and silk stockings; while they talked they also busily lashed the flies from their legs with their handkerchiefs. The flies were so bothersome, Jefferson said that the delegates finally decided to sign the Declaration of Independence at once and get away from the place as quickly as possible. Jefferson told the story "with much glee," said the friend; he was amused by the "influence of the flies" on so momentous an event.

Source: Mrs. E.F. Ellet, *The Court Circles of the Republic* (Hartford, Connecticut: Hartford Publishing Company, 1869), pp. 69-70.

On a visit home once, according to a popular story, Jefferson was out riding with some young men. They came across a rough-looking Kentuckian seated on the bank of a swollen stream waiting for somebody to give him a ride. The Kentuckian waited until everyone but Jefferson had entered the stream, then asked Jefferson to take him across. Jefferson gave him the ride. When he had safely deposited him on the opposite bank, one of the young men cried: "I say! What made you let the young men pass and ask that gentleman to carry you over the creek?" "Wall," said the Kentuckian, "If you want to know I'll tell you: I reckon a man carries yes or no in his face — the young chaps' faces said no — the old un's said yes." "It isn't every man that would have asked the President of the United States for a ride behind him," said the young man severly. The Kentuckian was astonished. "You don't say that was Tom Jefferson, do you?" he exclaimed. Then he added: "He's a ...fine old fellow, anyway." "That was the President," emphasized the young man. The Kentuckian thought for a minute, then burst out with a laugh: "What do you suppose my wife Polly, will say when I get back to Boone County, and tell her I've rid behind Jefferson? She'll say I voted for the right man!"

James Madison

Source: Francis J. Grund, *Aristocracy in America*, R. Bentley (London, New York), 1839, pp. 250-251.

When Madison was Secretary of State under Thomas Jefferson, a loyal Republican dropped into his office one day and asked to be governor of a western territory. Madison told him that other applicants had stronger claims. The man then asked for a collectorship. Unfortunately, Madison told him, they were all taken. "How about a post-office?" "Out of the question." "Well," said the man, "did the Secretary have any old clothes he could spare?"

John Quincy Adams

Source: Mrs. E. F. Ellet, *op. cit.*, pp. 129-130.

Both Josiah Quincy, President of Harvard, and John Quincy Adams rose very early in the morning; thus when they sat down for a minute or two later in the day they sometimes dozed off. One day the two of them went into Justice Joseph Story's classroom at Harvard to hear him lecture to his law students. The judge received them politely, placed them on the platform by his side, and began delivering his lecture. In a few minutes both of his visitors were sound asleep. Story stopped speaking and, pointing to Adams and Quincy, announced: "Gentlemen, you see before you a melancholy example of the evil effects of early rising!" The students' roar of laughter roused the slumberers, and Story then resumed his lecture.

Abraham Lincoln

Source: Keith W. Jennison, *The Humorous Mr. Lincoln* (New York: Cromwell, 1965), pp. 95-96.

When young Abraham Lincoln joined the Sangamon (Illinois) militia during the Black Hawk War, his colonel was a little fellow about four feet three inches tall. Lincoln was unusualy tall, but in those days, he tended to walk with a slouch. The colonel yelled at Lincoln for his sloppy posture. "Come on Abe," he cried, "hold up your head high fellow!" "Yes sir," said Abe. "High fellow," persisted the colonel. "Higher!" Abe straightened up, stretched his neck, and said, "So sir?" "Yes, fellow," said the colonel, "but a little higher." "And am I always to remain so?" asked Abe. "Yes, fellow, certainly," exclaimed the colonel. "Then," said Abe with a sad look, "goodbye colonel, for I shall never see you again."

Woodrow Wilson

Source: Faye and Lewis Copeland, editors, *1000 Jokes, Toasts, and Stories* (Garden City, New York: Halcyon House, 1940), p. 540.

Riding along a country road near Washington one day, accompanied by a Secret Service agent, President Wilson passed a small boy by the roadside. "Did you see what that boy did?" Wilson asked his companion. "No, sir," said the Secret Service agent; "what did he do?" "He made a face at me," said the President gravely. The Secret Service agent was shocked, but the President smiled and said, "Did you see what I did?" "No sir." "Well," said the President with a mischievous look, "I made a face right back at him."

Harry Truman

Source: Merle Miller, *Plain Speaking*, (New York: Gollancz, 1974), pp. 393-394.

Once when President Truman was visiting Kansas City, he invited Eddie Meissberger, a retired post office employee and a veteran of Battery D (Truman's World War I unit) for lunch. When Eddie arrived he found several other veterans of Battery D present. The President opened the drawer of a desk, grinned, went over and locked the door, got some tumblers from a cupboard, then took out a bottle and poured each of his friends a drink. "Where is your glass?" they asked him. Truman told them that he couldn't take a drink right then because in the next room was a delegation of Baptist ladies from Independence, Missouri, whom he had promised to see in a few minutes. "But," he said, "I have a bad cold coming on, and I'll just put this away and take it out at home tonight and use it." And he put the bottle back in the desk. Then Eddie said: "Well. I'm on a government payroll, you know, and I don't know whether I should take one right now." "Well," said Truman, "as President, I'll give you fifteen — fifteen minutes of annual leave right now, and you can join the others." So it was "down the hatch" for all of Truman's former buddies.

Source: Margaret Truman, *Harry S. Truman* (New York: Morrow, 1973), pp. 280-281.

When Truman went to the Potsdam Conference in July 1945, he took an old Missouri friend, Fred Canfil, with him. One day after a meeting, Truman called Canfil over and introduced him to Stalin. "Marshal Stalin," he said, "I want you to meet Marshal Canfil." Truman did not explain that he had recently made Canfil a federal marshal in Missouri. After that introduction, Canfil was treated with great respect by all the members of the Russian delegation.

Richard M. Nixon

Source: "Signing Off," *Reader's Digest*, LXXVII, November 1962, p. 330.

In 1962, when Nixon was autographing his book, *Six Crises*, in a California bookstore, he asked one purchaser to whom he should address his greeting. "You've just met your seventh crisis," said the customer. "My name is Stanislaus Wojechzleschki."

Ronald Reagan

Source: "Reagan's One-Liners," *The New York Times*, February 6, 1881, p. A13.

President Reagan turned seventy in February 1981 and joked about his age in a speech at a Washington Press Club dinner. "I know your organization was founded by six Washington newspaper men in 1919," he remarked; then, after a slight pause, added: "It seems like only yesterday." Middle age, he went on to say, "is when you're faced with two temptations and you choose the one that will get you home at 9 o'clock." And, after quoting Thomas Jefferson's advice not to worry about one's age, he exclaimed: "And ever since he told me that, I stopped worrying."

Source: "Seriously, Folks.....," *Time*, CXXXIII, April 13, 1981, p. 30.

President Reagan was famous for his one-liners. Even in emergencies he preserved his good humor and tossed off quip after quip to reassure those around him. An attempt on his life early in his Presidency left him as calm and unruffled as Theodore Roosevelt had been after a similar attack many years before. Reagan was rushed to the hospital with a serious chest wound, but when he was wheeled into the operating room, he grinned and told the surgeons: "Please assure me that you are all Republicans!" "Today," responded one of the doctors, "we're all good Republicans, Mr. President." A few hours after surgery the President wrote his doctors a note which parodied comedian W.C. Fields: "All in all, I'd rather be in Philadelphia." A little later he sent another note from the intensive care section to White House aides waiting outside: "Winston Churchill said: 'There's no more exhilarating feeling than being shot at without result.'" Two hours later came a third note: "If I had had this much attention in Hollywood, I'd have stayed there."

When doctors praised Reagan for being a good patient, he told them, "I have to be. My father-in-law is a doctor." To the nurse removing a trachea tube he said confidently: "I always heal fast." Said she: "Keep up the good work." "You mean this may happen several times more?" he cried in mock dismay. Greeting White House aides the morning after surgery, he exclaimed: "Hi, fellas. I knew it would be too much to hope that we could skip a staff meeting." Told that the Government was running smoothly while he was in the hospital, he pretended indignation: "What makes you think I'd be happy about that?" And when he heard about the progress being made by the other men who had been wounded in the assassination attempt, he exclaimed: "That's great news. We'll have to get four bedpans and have a reunion."

Political Anecdotes and Jokes

The next selection of anecdotes and jokes comes from another anthology, The Fun and Laughter of Politics, *by John F. Parker, Doubleday and Company, Garden City, New York, 1978. Parker was Minority Leader of the Massachusetts State Senate. He does not take credit for originating the anecdotes and jokes, rather, he collected them over the years from numerous politician friends.*

How To Tell Who Your Friends Are

Elliot Richardson, prior to becoming Attorney General under President Richard Nixon, was campaigning for the post of Lieutenant Governor of Massachusetts. Richardson continually told this story as a way of making a point.

A scoutmaster was giving a lecture to some scouts on the hazards of camping. "And, boys," warned the scoutmaster, "you must be careful of snakes. If one of these snakes happens to bite you on the hand, just take out your knife and crisscross the place where the snake bit you and suck out the poison. Are there any questions?"

A freckle-faced boy in the rear of the room raised his hand and asked: "Mr. scoutmaster, you say if a snake bites you on the hand, you cut it with a knife and suck out the poison? What do you do if a snake bites you on the rear end?"

"Well, I'll tell you son," replied the scoutmaster with a straight face, "that's when you find out who your friends are."

Who's Perfect

There was a great deal of graft during the Tammany Hall regime in New York City. A citizen approached a local politician one day and offered him a bribe for a political favor.

With apparent surprise, the politician responded: "I want you to know that as a public servant, I never take money for favors." Then, reaching for the money and putting it in his pocket, he added with a wink, "but who's perfect these days?"

A Lincoln Club Dinner

Senator Howard Baker of Tennessee was commenting on the growing lack of interest and knowledge in American history. He told of a plane trip he made to the West Coast to speak at a dinner honoring President Abraham Lincoln. On the flight to San Francisco, Baker became the center of attention because of his role in the Watergate hearings. A young lady asked him where he was going. "Oh," said Baker, "I'm on my way to San Francisco to speak at a Lincoln club dinner."

"San Francisco?" said the young lady. "Gee, my father lives in San Francisco and he owns a Lincoln. Maybe he'll be at the dinner."

Back to Farming

Soon after a drenching rain ended a Texas drought, this advertisement appeared in the local newspaper. "J.H. Hones withdraws his candidacy for Congressman. It has rained sufficiently for Mr. Hones to return to farming."

They Started to Boo Again

A young man gave his first political speech. Telling the story later, he said: "Ahead of me on the program was my opponent, who gave a long winded speech. The crowd started to hiss and boo until he could no longer continue. Then I came on for my speech. I was doing fine for about three minutes. Then, would you believe it, right in the middle of my speech, they started booing the first speaker all over again."

Lunatics and Fools

According to one Congressman there are two enemies to every bill proposed in Congress. The fools who favor it and the lunatics who oppose it.

A Laundry Bill

A popular story about the Massachusetts legislature centers on a laundry bill that was sent to the House of Representatives by mistake. When the manager of the laundry company noted the error, he immediately called the Clerk of the House and informed him that his billing department had forwarded a laundry bill to the Massachusetts House by mistake and would they please return it.

"It's too late," said the Clerk. "They have already passed it."

Another collection of anecdotes and jokes is Handbook of Humor *by Famous Politicians prepared by the Life Underwriters Political Action Committee, 1968. They asked Members of Congress to submit stories to them and the Political Action Committee (PAC) compiled the list. The following anecdotes and stories are selected from that compilation.*

Who Wants to Go First

The toasmaster was an old hand at the game and his head-line political speaker for the political dinner was going to be delayed. He was foresighted enough to have on the backup speaking program two young governors from neighboring states. He immediately launched into a glowing introduction, describing the "next speaker" as "one of the greatest chief executives in the history of his State, one of the finest men ever to hold a public office,...etc." He then stepped slightly back and said to his two young gubernatorial guests — in a voice which unfortunately was picked up by the sound system: "Which one of you guys wants to go first?"

Harry the Vendor

This story was submitted by former Governor Harold LeVander of Minnesota.

The President of Lakewood State Junior College was called from a faculty meeting to take an important phone call. His secretary rushed in and announced: "The governor wants to talk to you Dr. Hill!" A buzz went around the conference table.

"Wow, the governor."

Dr. Hill hurried to the telephone. "Yes governor, what can I do for you?"

"Governor?" asked the puzzled voice on the other end of the phone. "Say Dr. Hill, this is Harry the vendor. About that coffee machine in the basement...."

Harry the vendor was doubly puzzled by the laughter at the other end of the line (Governor Harold {Harry} LeVander — Harry the vendor).

He Lost All His Marbles

A young man wanted to become a politician. He knew that in order to succeed he would have to become a good speaker — so he decided to copy Diogenes, the famous Greek who had learned to speak by filling his mouth with pebbles, only he had to fill his mouth with marbles since he didn't have any pebbles. Each day he spoke with his mouth full of marbles and after each practice session he removed one marble. At the end he figured he was a good enough speaker to be a politician — he'd finally lost all his marbles.

Everyone Has the Right to Vote

There are times that a political candidate is accused of having too many votes in the ballot box. As a story in point, two congressional aides were out in a graveyard on a dark Saturday night before election day, getting names off of tombstones. One aide held a flashlight while the other aide had a pencil and notebook. They came to a name on a weathered marker and they couldn't read it. The aide with the notebook said: "Come on. We have enough names. Let's not spend any more time on this one." The other man replied, "Nope, we'll stay right here until we get his name. He has got just as much right to vote as the rest of them have."

Help Me Become a Citizen

A Congresssman who had just won a third term to Congress was approached on the street by a supporter. The supporter detailed how he always voted for the him. The Congressman thanked him warmly for his long-standing, firm support. The supporter continued: "Since I have always voted for you, I was wondering if you could do me a favor. Could you help me become a U.S. citizen?"

More Wit and Wisdom

A classic book on political humor was edited by Edward Boykin in 1961,
The Wit and Wisdom of Congress. *Following are several selections.*

Cure the Dog

Source: Edward Boykin, editor, *The Wit and Wisdom of Congress* (New York: Funk and Wagnall, 1961), p. 14.

Senator Shelby M. Cullom of Illinois commented in 1894:

It may be remembered that Horace Greeley once wrote a book entitled *What I Know About Farming*. Subsequently it became fashionable to perplex him with all sorts of queries about agriculture. One man wrote him inquiring the best way to cure a dog of killing sheep. Greeley promptly answered, "Cut off his tail just behind his ears." It seems to me, Mr. President, that the proper way to cure the Wilson bill which proposes to kill all the sheep in this country and rely upon other countries for wool, is to amputate this bill just below the enacting clause.

Angel or Elf?

"Sunset" Sam Cox, a Member of the House for thirty years, was a small man in size, but overpowering in his opinions. In the following excerpt, the 250-pound Representative from Michigan, Roswell G. Horr, who often disagreed with Cox, needled him as "my genial little friend" in

the debate over the Harbor and River Bill, in 1880. He proposed this epitaph for his colleague who had such a high opinion of himself:

Source: *Ibid.*, p. 69.

Beneath this slab lies the great SAM COX,
He was wise as an owl and grave as an ox;
Think it not strange his turning to dust,
For he swelled and he swelled till he finally "bust."
Just where he's gone or just how he fares
Nobody knows and nobody cares.
But wherever he is, be he angel or elf,
Be sure, dear reader, he's puffing himself.

It's All in the Way You Say It.

Representative W. Bourke Cockran of New York in 1906, had this to say about the English language.

Source: *Ibid.*, p. 21.

I do not know that I see before me one individual who I believe can write an English sentence of twenty words that I cannot give more than one meaning to. It is an exceedingly difficult thing to use the English language in such a way that ingenious carping cannot find fault with it. My friend here has undoubtedly heard the story of the little girl who at her prayers in the morning said, "Good-by, God; We are going to move to Missouri." Her wicked brother, who happened to overhear her, and who was jubilant at the idea of the journey, used the very same sentence, but he said, "Good! By God, we are going to move to Missouri!"

They Laughed in December 1899

Source: *Ibid.*, p. 110.

John J. Fitzgerald of Massachusetts was not elected to Congress for his ability as a prophet, but he apparently struck a vein in the last sentence of his salutation to the departing Nineteenth Century.

Think for a moment what a hundred years has brought forth. This century received from its predecessor the horse; we bequeath the bicycle, the locomotive, and the automobile. We received the goosequill; we bequeath the typewriter. We received the scythe; we bequeath the mowing machine. We received the sickle; we bequeath the harvester. We received the hand printing press; we bequeath the Hoe cylinder press. We received painted canvas; we bequeath lithography, photography, and color photography. We received the cotton and wool loom; we bequeath the factory.

We received gunpowder; we bequeath nitroglycerine. We received the tallow dip; we bequeath the arc light. We received the flintlock; we bequeath the automatic firing gun. Receiving nothing, we bequeath the anaesthetic properties of sulphur ether, by means of which to a great extent human life has been saved and pain prevented. We received the beacon signal; we bequeath the telephone and wireless telegraphy. We received ordinary light; we bequeath the X-ray. We received the old-fashioned sailing ship; we bequeath the ocean greyhound and freight leviathan.

Perhaps with the coming of the twentieth century airships may be invented to sail from this country to other parts of the world. (Laughter)

Suggested Further Reading

Anderson Jack. *Alice in Blunderland*. Washington, D.C., Acropolis Books, 1983.

Beard, Henry. *The Official Politically Correct Dictionary and Handbook*. New York, Villard Books, 1992.

Boykin, Edward, editor. *The Wit and Wisdom of Congress*. New York: Funk and Wagnalls Company, 1961.

Combs, James E. *The Comedy of Democracy*. Westport, Conn. Praeger, 1996.

Domke, Todd. *The Conservative's Dictionary*. New York, St. Martin's Griffin, 1996.

Franken, Al. *Rush Limbaugh is a Big Fat Idiot and Other Observations*. Thorndike, ME., Thorndike Press, 1996.

Fun and Laughter of Politics, compiled by John F. Parker, Garden City, N.Y., Doubleday, 1978.

Gardner, Gerald C. *All the Presidents' Wits*. New York, Beech Tree Books, 1986.

Gottlieb, Alan M. *Politically Correct Environment*. Bellevue, WA, Merril Press, 1996.

Hyman, Dick. *Washington Wit and Wisdom*. Lexington, Mass., S. Greene Press, 1988.

Jackley, John L. *Below the Beltway*. Washington, D.C., Regnery Publishers, 1996.

Keefe, William J. *Impurely Academic*. New Brunswick, N.J., Transaction Books, 1980.

Lawless, Ken. *Who's the Next President*. New York, Perigee Books, 1988.

Moser, Edward P. *The Politically Correct Guide to American History*. New York, Crown Publisher, 1996.

Shaw, David. *The Pleasure Police*. New York, Doubleday, 1996.

Stout, Joseph, Jr. editor. *Convention Articles of Will Rogers*. Stillwater, OK, Oklahoma State University Press, 1976.

Twain, Mark. *The Political Tales and Truth of Mark Twain*. San Rafael, CA, New World Library, 1992.

Walker, Robert Martin. *Politically Correct Parables*. Kansas City, MO, Andrews and McMeel, 1996.

About the Editor

Stephen M. Forman is the author of *A Guide to Civil War Washington, Abraham Lincoln's Washington* (map), *The Cold War*, and numerous articles on the Civil War and American history. He is a writer, educator, and licensed tour guide. Steve is a regular contributor to the *Washington Times'* Civil War page. He was a high school teacher in New York City, taught at George Washington University, and currently teaches an off-campus seminar, "The Development of Washington D.C." for visiting educators at the United States Naval Academy. He is the historian at Congressional Cemetery, the nation's first national cemetery. Forman is on the Board of Faculty Advisors for the Civil War Education Association and a consultant for education program development for the American Blue & Gray Association. He is a tour guide and program developer for the Smithsonian Institution and a tour guide/lecturer for The Capitol Historical Society, and Ford's Theater National Historic Site. He speaks and lectures throughout the United States. Steve is also the editor of companion volumes in this *Perspectives on History Series*, *Echoes of the Civil War: The Gray*, and *Echoes of the Civil War: The Blue*.